Kaplan Classes:
Prepare to score your highest on the PSAT,* SAT,* or ACT* !

Take Kaplan and get the score you need to get into college. Our score-raising method identifies your strengths and weaknesses, builds your knowledge and provides you with the skills, stamina, and confidence needed to score your absolute best. And, Kaplan's PSAT, SAT, and ACT courses are taught by expert teachers who use proven test-taking techniques. Taking a Kaplan course is easy. Kaplan offers a full schedule of classes during the day, in the evening, and on weekends at over 1,200 locations nationwide.

Call today to enroll.

World Leader in Test Prep

1-800-KAP-TEST

kaptest.com AOL keyword: kaplan

Applying to College?

We've got some recommended reading.

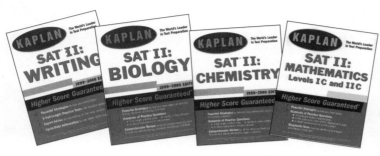